FLOWER ARRANGEMENT

through the year

Other books by Violet Stevenson
DRIED FLOWERS FOR DECORATION
THE ENCYCLOPAEDIA OF FLORISTRY
THE ENCYCLOPAEDIA OF CHRISTMAS AND FESTIVAL DECORATIONS
THE FLOWER ARRANGER'S GARDEN
FLOWER DECORATION FOR THE HOME
INDIVIDUAL FLOWERS
LONG LASTING FLOWER ARRANGEMENTS
SIMPLE FLOWER ARRANGEMENT
TAKE THREE FLOWERS

FLOWER

ARRANGEMENT

through the year

by

Violet Stevenson

W H & L Collingridge Ltd
London

To

E. D. DUGE

who has taught so many

children to see with

new eyes

First published in 1952
by W. H. & L. Collingridge Ltd
Tower House, Southampton St
London, W.C.2
Printed in Great Britain by
Balding & Mansell Ltd
Wisbech
Fourth Revised Edition 1966
© Violet Stevenson 1966

THE FLOWER ARRANGEMENTS

The numbers in this list refer to the photographic plates

INTRODUCTION

MODERN FLOWER ARRANGEMENT is the new domestic art. The vase of mixed home-grown flowers has taken the place of the sampler. Colours, shapes and patterns are intermingled and blended with all the love, skill and understanding that was once applied to tapestry.

I am glad that it has been called an art and not a science for it is an art although there are those who would set the marriage of vase and flowers on a plane with geometry, confined by mathematical formulae. Arranging flowers gives us a chance to handle colour, to observe shapes, to create patterns and harmonies – things that many of us stop doing once we have left school and the art class.

Flower arrangement is for everyone. It need not and indeed should not be confined to those who have a large and well-stocked garden complemented by a collection of choice vases and space to store them. But we find that although there are many delightful books on the subject little has been written solely for the townswoman, the flat-dweller, for the many who have only a tiny garden or none at all and who have little to spend on decorative materials; for those who must go for them to the local florist, the street seller or even the hedgerow.

We find that these people who are dependent on commercially produced flowers are often discouraged and disinclined to experiment further with flower arrangement. Those who grow all their own materials may not realize that the carefully cultivated, perfectly uniform, mass-produced blooms of our flower markets are not the easiest materials to arrange. With a little coaxing the trailing rose or twisted snapdragon fall obligingly into exciting line patterns. Not so the flowers in a bunch of daffodils or chrysanthemums. Straight-stemmed, uniform flowers need a special technique, one that makes allowances for perfection yet must strive to mask it.

But even more exasperating are fast-fading flowers which are such a disappointment to the arranger who has to buy every bloom. Fortunately, commercial flower growers have now realized that the best way to sell more flowers is to get them to the ultimate customer in as young a state as possible. As I write, almost all spring flowers raised from bulbs are being gathered and marketed in the bud stage by more and more growers. Thus the arranger can watch the flowers open from the time they are brought into the home instead of, as was once the case, watching them die. I believe that before long we shall see this practice extended to flowers other than those grown from bulbs.

Flowers in bud need no different arrangement from any other type of flower. All that is necessary is that one should realize that the flowers must have room to develop and to space them accordingly.

I hope to show in this book how these commercial flowers on which so many of us depend for our decoration may be arranged into pleasing patterns, combinations, contrasts and harmonies. In almost every arrangement the flowers used may be replaced by others of similar shape or colour. The 'pattern' of arrangement for one flower, say the chrysanthemum, may be adapted for many other round flowers, for instance, dahlias, roses, or even daisies. It is not always possible to buy accessories, leaves and grasses, but I have tried to show which are readily available. Many of them may be used several times.

The arrangements are not intended to be show pieces. They are decorations for the home throughout the year. They have been enjoyed in my home and I hope that through their example other homes will become more beautiful and other people happier. Yet please do not take these as models. Flower arrangement depends upon the personality of the individual and the pictures that follow are merely examples of my own tastes in decoration.

You will find that the same vase has been used more than once. This again is designed. I have an enormous collection of flower vases but I have friends who have no more than three. So again, the types of container are as restricted as the flowers.

Not one flower has been grown by me. Living in the heart of London as I do every flower has to be bought. But I never make an excursion without bringing home something to supplement my 'sophisticates'. Those most easily found are shown in these pages.

V.S.

Snowdrops are the essence of simplicity – perfectly suited to an unsophisticated style of arrangement. In a tiny rough pottery bowl holding a ball of wire netting screwed-up tightly these have been allowed to fall quite naturally. All stems appear to spring from the same point, the tallest stems being placed first. Treat any small flowers in this way.

I

Above: The contrasting colour for the sweetly scented Soleil d'Or, one of our earliest narcissi, comes from a few aucuba leaves, blue muscari, two mauve anemones and a bright copper skillet. *Right:* In this arrangement pastel-tinted tulips are arranged before three *Begonia rex* leaves in a queen conch shell. The three buds are new but the shortened flowers are a fortnight old.

4

Left: Modern line arrangement is just the thing for scarce winter flowers. South African chincherinchees, Icelandic reindeer moss and individual evergreen leaves are all long lasting. The camellia may be substituted as it fades by any short-stemmed flower, or posy of small flowers. The tallest stem should be placed first to set the pattern for design. The metal vase is raised to give extra height. *Below:* Flowers are often more effective when grouped. Colour is more intense too as we see in the analogous harmony of coral *Chaenomeles speciosa* (the Japonica), yellow catkins and orange calendulas in a green bowl. See how the calendulas form a curve and not a harsh line.

5

JANUARY

Above: Freesias are long lasting, their buds opening well in water. A bunch of twelve may seem meagre, but the flowers can be attractively arranged with seasonal materials for additional emphasis. The tall, narrow-necked vase lends itself to a spreading design. With the freesias are three sprays of *Prunus triloba* – alternatively use pussy willow – two sprays of ivy pulled from a tree, two sprays of grey-green eucalyptus saved from a previous arrangement, and a few variegated leaves which may also be saved and used again. Tall stems were first held in the hand and tied together. Short stems should be allowed to curve as they will, below rim level if possible. *Right:* Freesias look delightful in glass and in this case I have taken a little green storage jar from the bathroom to hold them. The tall stems have a skirt of marbled cyclamen leaves which also aid arrangement, and a few chlorophytum leaves make up for the lack of the flower's own foliage. The jar top is filled with damp Oasis so no water can be spilled.

6

Below: Forced lilies-of-the-valley have an ethereal ballerina-like quality. Each bell is silhouetted above a mass of grey reindeer moss. This filled the pewter salt cellar and held the grouped violet and primrose stems in place. Each silky lily leaf has been used, the chartreuse green a wonderful complement to the violet. *Right:* This is one of my favourite arrangements, chiefly because the characteristic stiffness of the bulbous flowers has been cloaked by dainty trails of ivy, pittosporum and pussy willow. The tallest flowers at the back are raised in a plastic tooth brush tube filled with water.

8

9

Left: If we arrange daffodils just as they grow we lose much of their colour value. However, in this flower-pot-like vase they have been placed quite informally and as naturally as possible. Mimosa and freesias add colour and variety. All stems radiate from the centre. The lower leaves are those of pittosporum, an attractive shade of green. *Above:* Arrangements should not be high if your rooms are low. Use a long container and arrange the flowers at an angle with the central upright stem not too high. Lilac is cut down almost to the height of the narcissi. Yellow-spotted evergreen aucuba leaves veil the stiff bare stems and do away with the need for many short-stemmed flowers at the base.

MARCH-APRIL

Left: Any flowers that have survived from a former design may be supplemented with new companions. The mauve and copper freesias taken from a mixed bunch are interspersed between the week-old yellow tulips. Ivy and philodendron, picked from house plants, repeat the green of the tulip leaves and bring an air of freshness. For such an arrangement start from the base, using a pinholder, and work up to the tallest flowers.

Below: A different style for a long, low arrangement composed of one bunch of Pheasant Eye narcissi (*Narcissus poeticus*) and pussy willow sprigs. Wire netting holds the stems. The 'plinth' is an ash tray turned upside down. Bulb flowers last best when arranged in shallow water but make sure that they are first given a long drink for several hours in deep water.

13

Above: Spring flowers have strong personalities and are the most difficult to mix. It is easiest to group them as they grow, in little families. Mass some for colour value but do not smother the irises. They are the fleurs-de-lis. Imagine them embroidered on a banner! *Right:* A small handful of flowers makes a fairly large decoration in an upright vase, tall stems at the back. Short flowers are best first bunched, tied, then placed at rim level. Soft pussy willow spread out to the sides makes the decoration wider. Alternatively, use blossom, newly budded twigs or fruit tree prunings. Flowers with well-defined centres or 'eyes' are best placed at the heart of any mixed arrangement.

APRIL-MAY

16

Left: Lively contrasts may be achieved with form or colour. A bunch of irises has been transformed by shells and willow. The stems are held on a pinholder placed between the shells. The willow is fixed in modelling clay. More shells are strewn over the floor of the container, an oval oven dish. *Below:* White lilac and pink tulips in a black vase offer a refreshing change. The heavy trusses are easily arranged if they are allowed to fall to the left or right. Trim sprigs from too heavy branches and arrange elsewhere in a low dish. Smash the ends of the stems and remove foliage to prevent flagging.

MAY-
JUNE

18

Left: Any one flower style is not suitable for every setting. Contemporary furnishings need clean-cut arrangements with the accent on purity of line. The wrong style of design can be as discordant as an antimacassar on a Clive Latimer chair. Shown here is a single arrangement of calla lilies (*Zantedeschia aethiopica*). *Above:* The arrangement of daisies, beech and hawthorn, which can be reproduced throughout the season with any 'round' flowers and foliage frame, is based on traditional massed design and looks well in most English settings. The glass vase has been stippled with shoe white to match the flowers and hide the ugly mass of stripped stems. Flowers of both arrangements are held in wire netting. The bunch of daisies, *Chrysanthemum maximum*, was placed in position after the beech leaves.

20 *Above:* The container should be an integral part of a flower arrangement, either so self-effacing that it is as inconspicuous as the soil in which a plant grows, or specially selected to suit the colour or form of the flowers. This shell was chosen because it is similar in shape to the sweet pea flowers, whose standard petal is fluted like the fan of the shell. Its aperture was packed with wet porous Florapak and the stems arranged in it. Side stems were placed first. If you look round you will find that many of the best containers are near at hand. *Right:* Roses are arranged in a kitchen jar. The handle is hidden, so is the word 'sugar'. If roses have stiff, straight stems, curves have to be artificially achieved by cutting them. Note how the graded centre flowers curve down into a reversed J. Try this arrangement with any straight-stemmed round flower.

Bowls are popular containers and there are many ways of using them. *Below:* This arrangement of six roses in smoky Swedish glass is not a far step from a 'floating' bowl. It is ideal if you have only a few flowers for the table. The stems are anchored by a little ball of wire netting hooked by two or more of its cut ends over the side of the bowl. Any short-stemmed flower may be used in this way with plenty of foliage to hide the wire. Of course, much depends on the beauty of the bowl. *Right:* The pewter fruit bowl holds a mixture of red and rose pyrethrums and the stems of some of these have been cut short. The cut portion is used among the flowers to hide the netting. It is not necessary to change the water daily, only to top it up. The portion of stem which goes under water must be stripped of leaves which otherwise would decompose unpleasantly.

22

23

MAY-
JUNE

The cheapest flowers are often most effective. Sometimes they need a little grooming. Faded blooms should be nipped out. Underwater stems of gypsophila must be stripped quite clean. Additional height has been achieved by using the tooth brush tube again. The black plinth under the vase adds another two inches.

SPRING: Mass-produced flowers are uniform but their formality can be exploited in many ways. Here a dozen tulips have been fanned – but not too severely – for the few blooms out of line eliminate stiffness. The downward flow of the catkins and the open-hearted cabbage bring contrasting shape, texture and colour. They also help to furnish the vase.

SUMMER: Pyrethrums give good value, usually outliving other flowers in a mixed arrangement. While they are in colour harmony with the pyrethrums the sweet peas also bring scent. The statice provides a contrast in shape. Morning glories (which came from the author's roof garden in this case) need to be picked in bud and replaced daily.

25

The underlying gold pattern in the cloth prompted this rose table decoration. Croton leaves, yellow and orange, bring colour that glows under artificial light. The grasses are bleached barley. The container is a tin-lined gilded basket. The stems extended at each side give extra length. Long pointed leaves were also placed at these points.

Above: Lovely leaves not only enhance the colour of flowers but they help to furnish a vase, and being long-lasting they are very economical. This hosta foliage may be used many times. At present it is complementary to the vivid vermilion of Super Star roses and Spitfire gladioli. *Right:* Roses may be broken down and used in this way in a jug or pewter tankard. Place the lower stems in position first and gradually build up the arrangement. Buds placed at the extremities of the arrangement give an effective finish.

26

28

Above: Fragrant white Regal lilies have rosy-purple flushed backs to the petals which I have matched with luscious cherries. These are framed against deep wine-red croton and green hosta leaves. There were man flowers to one of the lily stems so several were cut and arranged lov *Right:* For smaller decorations spiky stems may be cut down and placed i a definite pattern. The outline and colour of these liatris, held on a pir holder, reflect those of the *Begonia rex* leaves. The spikes flower from th tip downwards.

JULY

3

Most flower arrangements fall into a pattern. These are both triangular but one stands high and one low. Curving stems help to dispel any stiffness. *Left:* The scabious, flowers and buds, have been encouraged to curve. The gladioli are set well in among the other flowers so that there will be no great gap as their lower spike flowers fade. Some spiky leaves are used to fill in the outline. Vivid orange calendulas and scarlet roses are grouped centrally. *Below:* A gift of a little garden posy also presented problems since many of the stems were so short. However, a few sprigs of candlewick statice gave height and colour. The catmint, left and right, is excellent material for tapering.

31

JULY - AUGUST

3^2

Daisies have strong personalities and arranged with other flowers are inclined to steal the limelight. Place them then at the heart of an arrangement to form a focal point. For a basket container the same rules apply as for vase arrangements. The materials are best grouped. Blooms here have been eked out with harmonizing foliage. *Left:* Arranged here with golden coreopsis and statice are stems of golden privet. Round the centre daisy is a tuft of lamb's ear, *Stachys lanata.* The dried water grass and rue adds height. *Below:* An 'egg' of screwed-up wire netting pushed on a lump of modelling clay holds these China asters. Copper beech gives a glorious colour contrast. Use has been made of every bud, including one or two Michaelmas daisies.

33

34

Above: When flowers are uniform, even stiff, their formality can be exploited. A bunch of twelve *Chrysanthemum maximum* Esther Read are arranged in a triangle. Stems of wheat, wild vetch and golden privet break the stiffness and create colour harmony – black, green, gold and white. *Right:* Flowers grouped like the zinnias give a concentration of colour. The stems are stiff but this quality has been exploited.

AUGUST-SEPTEMBER

Left: Materials collected on a walk can provide a valuable colour contribution to any arrangement. These bryony berries keep well in or out of water. The trails should be cut into convenient lengths. Among the dried beech and hydrangea they ring a lively note. Fresh green bryony leaves arranged with them will turn yellow later. *Below:* The bright green, yellow and orange berry motley harmonizes well with the gold of the pompon dahlias. All stems are in wire netting.

38

AUGUST-SEPTEMBER

Left: As you have seen, patterns for flower arrangement are limitless. A nest of white-lined brown dishes prompted the design on the left. Water is in the centre dish only. A pinholder, well hidden by leaves and buds, holds the half moon of buff dahlias. *Above:* An unusual flower colour harmony is composed of mauve Climax Michaelmas daisies and matching anemones whose black centres are reflected in the gleaming wild privet berries and black glass vase. Berried stems need considerable grooming if they are to be dainty.

Almost the same materials have been used as in the arrangement shown on the previous page, yet a primrose-coloured bowl and sprays of light-hued *Aster ericoides* effectively change the colour harmony. Long side stems placed at right angles alter the shape and character of the arrangement. The flowers are easiest to handle if these are placed first. They should be held firmly in a ball of wire netting. Short-stemmed daisies are the laterals taken from a tall stem.

AUTUMN: In spite of its garden atmosphere everything in this arrangement except the fluffy wild clematis came from the florists. Spray chrysanthemums and hemerocallis were divided to provide both tall and short-stemmed flowers. When the colours in an arrangement are as vivid as these dahlias, gentians and the matching vase, and when the foliage is also pretty, few blooms prove to be plenty.

WINTER: Red, gold and green is a cheerful colour scheme for winter days, and fortunately there is a good seasonal choice for the flower arranger. These bright anemones were part of a mixed bunch. The crowded stems of red holly berries which surround them glow all the brighter because most of their leaves have been snipped away.

A permanent arrangement may be built up slowly as the materials are collected. Stems may be held in wire netting, sand or dry Florapak. The colour of hydrangea heads for drying should be changing from summer colours to the green and wine of autumn. These and the *Buddleia globosa* leaves need no preparation and may be placed in the vase at once. The spiky materials are seed heads of spiraea cut from a pot plant. The statice is yellow as mauve looks too dull among the broken colours of the other materials. This and the straw flowers, helichrysums, should be hung, head downwards, in a cool, dry place so that the blooms dry and the stems stiffen.

September-October

September-October

Left: Orange, white and green. Fresh and dried materials together have an unusual yet satisfying quality. The silvery moons of honesty are natural, but are sold dyed in several colours. The Chinese lanterns, physalis, matching the gladioli, are freshly gathered and still retain some leaves but they should be removed as they fade. Both these materials may be used again and again. The snowberry, *Symphoricarpos racemosus*, lasts well in water. The box leaves are exceptionally long lived and may be used again. *Below:* This is a favourite posy ring which lends itself to all kinds of decoration and is just big enough for a tea table or desk arrangement. One dahlia, five leaves, a little thuja and bright rose hips are held in wire netting.

43

Above: Blackberry leaves and fruits, privet berries, and chamomile prompted this yellow, white and black arrangement, perfect for a modern setting. White Michaelmas daisies and golden rod eke out the wild materials. *Right:* Used as it grows, pampas grass is suitable only for out-size decorations, but if the plumes are pulled apart they provide ideal complementary curving materials for stiff autumn flowers. These single yellow spray chrysanthemums are in a pale green modern pottery vase. The tallest stems have been 'lifted' by a tooth brush tube. Low central blooms were taken from the trusses and arranged separately. The grass may be used many times.

September-October

45

Left: Pompon chrysanthemums, like these blooms of Janté Wells grouped in a matching yellow bowl, are sometimes difficult to arrange. They are best pulled apart. Allow some to remain on long stems, from which all else is stripped, to be placed at the edges. Others, shorter stemmed, may in their turn be divided. Extra heavy trusses may be placed at rim level. Any flower, blossom, or berry, when arranged in this way, will give good colour value. *Above:* Fruits, leaves and flowers may be mixed for autumn and winter. The brightly coloured gourds are laid on flat rhododendron, coloured ivy and croton leaves. The stems of carnations are in a hidden bottle of water. The flowers should be changed as they fade and more re-arranged on the semi-permanent frame of fruit and leaves in the oven dish. Arrangements of this kind are ideal for the table.

48

OCTOBER

Left: This arrangement based on traditional design should look well in most settings. The container, a copper jelly mould, has been raised on an upturned dish for extra height. Sprays of bronze chrysanthemums were divided so that the flowers might be placed at different levels. The ornamental gourds match their green and yellow centres. If desired, gourds may be varnished to help them last longer but unless they are badly bruised they should see the winter through as they are. *Below:* Wild and cultivated materials mix well if all are in character. Most of the 'rules' of flower arrangement are broken here but the composition remains one of my favourites. Pompon chrysanthemums and Michaelmas daisies are set in crescents against pressed sweet chestnut leaves. Materials include elderberry, hips, haws, wild clematis, bryony and privet.

49

Above: This mixture was gathered from a garden but a walk along a lane will be just as richly if differently rewarded. The beauty of an arrangement of this kind is that one can keep adding to it, removing faded materials and replacing them with fresh. Even coloured leaves of some vegetables – beet, carrot or kale – may be used. Every bud is precious. *Right:* Wild or cultivated, summer- or winter-flowering heather makes attractive decorations. The stems should be placed in water or, alternatively, heather will dry and remain colourful. The colours do not fade so quickly if the cut stems are arranged in a potato! Use heather among 'permanent' arrangements as well as statice and the rest. It may be arranged out of water here, in wire netting, sand or Florapak.

50

52

Above and right: The 'stems' of these straw flowers, helichrysums, are straws cut from the shortened bleached barley. First make a hole with a knitting needle in the centre of the flowers. Insert the straw thin end first and pull through until the bloom is firm. Bracken should be gathered before it becomes curled but after it has turned colour. Place it flat between newspapers under the carpet to press and dry. It may be bought dyed and preserved. Materials are held in dry Florapak. No wires are needed. As this type of arrangement is so light, use a heavy container.

OCTOBER - NOVEMBER

OCTOBER - NOVEMBER

Left: In winter liven a dried arrangement with scarlet anemones held in a glass tube filled with water. The flowers may be changed as they fade and replaced by more blooms, berries, or coloured fresh foliage. *Below:* An all-the-year-round decoration may be made from leaves of all kinds, hardy and exotic mixed together. In winter dried leaves may form the framework for fresh materials. Arrange them as though they were flowers, tall stems at the back, vivid colours at the heart. This last is most important as colour provides the essential element.

55

Above: Mixed leaves have a hint of the Japanese style arranged in this way on a pinholder in a low pedestal bowl. *Right:* An uninspired market bunch of flowers needs new companions, though, to give it character. The pressed chestnut leaves match the flowers, while the buds, green leaves and stems provide contrast. Graceful seed heads of wall lettuce, *Prenanthes muralis*, can be gathered already dry almost anywhere.

NOVEMBER

58

Left: Flower arrangement should not be too serious a business. If you are having a party a little bit of nonsense like Dobbin here will provide an opening gambit for conversation. The vase behind him has ample room for the tufts of grey reindeer moss that hold the thin stems of the shell-pink quill chrysanthemums in place. The stems of barley all curving alike, with the wind as it were, give a quality of movement to the arrangement and are as much fun as the container. *Above:* Georgian pewter salt cellars hold winter gleanings from warmer days. These are miniatures but the same idea may be adopted for larger and more sweeping arrangements. Evergreens which need replacing only seldom form a frame for colourful snippets from hedgerows, shrubs, pot plants and dried materials. Pairs are particularly suitable for mantels and sideboards.

59

60 *Above:* Most well-grown chrysanthemums are so perfectly uniform that they resemble coloured washing-up mops and are just as difficult to arrange informally. However, foliage is always plentiful and may be used to conceal harsh lines. Six single blooms, which by themselves would make little show in a glass bowl, are fluffed out with preserved beech and golden cupressus. *Right:* The bunch of six double salmon-pink chrysanthemum blooms has been supplemented with tall soft grey grevillea or silk-bark oak leaves. These may be bought in natural hue or dyed in several colours. They dry well and may be used repeatedly.

NOVEMBER

Left: Carnations are not so expensive as they seem. Fresh flowers – the centre petals should be clustered tight and the outer petals bent down at right angles to the stem – should last well. Framed by turkey oak – the shade of the orange flakes in the carnation petals – the five blooms look important and the arrangement is made much taller. The pillow vase is one I designed to be placed quite near or flat against a wall. A hole in the the front allows one to arrange stems at a low level. *Above:* Candles add colour when flowers are scarce. They also provide height and line. Inserted in wire netting or Florapak they can be placed in bowls for the table centre or in long troughs for a buffet. The magenta candle harmonizes with the selected anemones.

Above: In winter evergreens come into their own. Use them freely with flowers. Neither will harm the other. For a table decoration multi-hued anemones may be mixed in a yellow teapot with golden curly cupressus – cheerful contrasting colour. *Right:* One bunch of anemones may be divided and used in several arrangements. In the brass beggar's bowl are just three blooms with good clusters of carefully saved bryony berries before a frame of one branch of flat-growing thuja.

64

DECEMBER

65

DECEMBER

Above: Cyclamen are perfect cut flowers but be sure first to cut away any curved portion at the base of the stems or they may not take water. Mine are arranged in a deep bowl-shaped ash tray. Glossy ivy leaves from the woods provide a strong foil for the flowers and hide the holder. Of course, cyclamen leaves may be used if you have them. *Right:* Two scarlet anemones taken from a bunch as suggested on p. 64, or in fact almost any small round flower, may be replaced when necessary. The black privet berries, matching the gleaming vase, broom, old man's beard and rhododendron leaves will last much longer.

66

67

A few ideas for Christmas decorations *Left:* A triangular pattern, based on the shape of the Christmas tree itself, consists of golden cupressus, laurustinus, beech and bryony berries. An arrangement of this kind will last for several weeks. If during the festivities you forget to keep the vase filled with water the materials will not quickly show signs of deterioration. Strip the lower one-third of stem. You will then be able to arrange a mass of materials in a narrow-necked container. *Below:* In a French glass vase, two sprays of thuja, white or red carnations and golden holly form a much daintier decoration with only the faintest seasonal hint about it, this being provided, of course, by the holly. Without this it remains just another idea for winter decoration.

70 *Above:* As a container for a Christmas table decoration use any dish, date box, cake tin or bowl, filled with damp moss, Florapak or tightly screwed wire netting. No water is used. Place the candle upright. Fix it in a lump of modelling clay if moss is used. Next, place in position the flat sprays of frosted bracken, fir or yew. Group all the materials round the candle. Strip and slant all stem ends so that they pierce the moss easily. Place the flowers direct in damp Florapak or, alternatively, in water in a pill tube. *Right:* This tall decoration will last long after Christmas. The green materials have their stems in water.

One of winter's compensations – Christmas roses (*Helleborus niger*). They are seldom sold with leaves attached but most green foliage will suit them. A snippet of pittosporum, individual leaves or trails of ivy are used here but I think they look sad with yew. Give the flowers a deep drink and always cut a fraction away from the base of the stem before arranging them.